A RUSH OF HANDS

Camino del Sol

A Latina and Latino Literary Series

Juan Delgado

A

RUSH

OF

HANDS

The University of Arizona Press ★ Tucson

The University of Arizona Press
Manufactured in the United States of America

08 07 06 05 04 03   6 5 4 3 2 1

LIBRARY OF CONGRESS CATALOGING-IN-PUBLICATION DATA

Delgado, Juan, 1960–
    A rush of hands / Juan Delgado.
      p. cm. — (Camino del sol)
    ISBN 0-8165-2255-3 (acid-free paper)
    1. Mexican Americans—Poetry. I. Title. II. Series.

    PS3554.E442465 R87 2003
    811'.54—dc21

                                                    2002011023

BRITISH LIBRARY CATALOGUING-IN-PUBLICATION DATA
A catalogue record for this book is available from the British Library.

Publication of this book is made possible in part by the proceeds of a
permanent endowment created with the assistance of a Challenge Grant
from the National Endowment for the Humanities, a federal agency.

To Larry

CONTENTS

A RUSH OF HANDS

Grandma Taught Me to Respect You

You had a cricket's body
A demon's skull,
And a line of corn for teeth.
You squatted, smiling at me,
Occupying me while Grandma
Told me another story.

You were all legs,
A spider under my bed,
Waiting until I fell asleep.
Her story was your web.

Once you found a boy
Walking through a graveyard
And caught his coat with a branch;
Your hooked finger froze the boy,
Afraid to turn and see you tugging.

You were king to kings
With your special crown,

A banana leaf, eggshell smooth.
You appeared above me,
A full moon startling me
Like my grandma's voice.

The Ward's Roosters

For JMD

I preferred you pacing the yard naked,
Pruning your roses at midnight by flashlight,
To the man I visited on Saturdays who eyed
The number on his wristband, a code,
A prescribed routine of pills and therapy.
I preferred the father who decided one night
To break all of our neighbor's flower pots,
Freeing the roots from their clay cages.
When they committed you to a mental ward,
I saw my shadow vanish like Peter Pan's.
Two fences surrounded the county hospital,
And driving by them, I pressed on the gas,
Watching the coils of barbed wire worm.
The questions I had about your illness
Dangled like the vines on the security gate.
You had had an episode, so they had canceled
Your visiting hours, and I drove to a parking lot
And slept in my car, waxed into a red apple
For a high school girl I had started to date.
I phoned, asking for you in the morning.

★

Spider webs, gas meters, sprinklers, my visits,

Dripping faucets, lunch bells—you used anything

You could to measure your passing days.

After they had you swallow your medicine,

Your mouth and tongue hardened, cement-slow,

Your eyes in a glare, a sidewalk's broken glass.

In the smoke of my weed I wore those eyes,

And sitting in my car I rested and dreamt:

The stockings of a nurse paced by your bathtub;

Her gloved hand reached down, pulling the plug.

The panic and illness in your head swirled, dirt

Snaking down the drain, funneling through

The hospital's pipes, then spilling into the gutter,

Mixing with a stream of clippings and grass.

You dressed in a suit and checked yourself out,

And when you crossed the yard to the gate,

The sprinklers popped out, the ward's roosters.

They spread a tiny rainbow among themselves,

And pinches of bread lay ahead of you.

El Caballo de Cortés

His flagship hoists its flags,
Casting a shadow,
A rising tower on the water.

      They disembark.
Dressed with a breastplate
And bells attached to its mane,
His horse trots and traps
A fly behind its eyelashes.

      A world flutters,
Caught in the rider's vision
        That goes beyond
The mountains and sunset.

The Ghost of Sal

One off-line headlight notices
The painted tar on the asphalt cracks
Then the moon shining on Sal's shoes.

After a long sleep a train passes
And leaves a wire dancing on the tracks,
A question mark fishing in the air.

He walks on the loose gravel,
Following along the tracks,
Looking to bum a smoke.

On his head he sports a panty hose,
Cut and tied in a knot, a rose for the chicas
Fashioned into his nylon crown.

He stops at the downtown wishing well
And flips in a coin, its face drifts to the other faces
Looking up at Sal's torso, coffin-framed.

★

His bleached T-shirt is a mark
For the car with a half-opened window,
Scoping his strut and calavera cap.

He is in the avocado grove, taking a leak.
He vanishes like the rising steam of his piss.
He doesn't care about his chicas' desires;
He doesn't care about anyone's desires.

Shrine

Another cross by the roadside,
This one, so like the others,
Has a rosary draped over the arms,
A bundle of stems.
A few wilted petals cling,
And five candles circle the cross,
Reminders of the drive-by shooting.
Only the phone number
Written in silver duct tape
On the cardboard box, a plea
For "Info," is unusual.
You have to do more than that,
More than chapter and verse,
Numbers leading some of us
Nowhere, and others to a place
All too familiar to revisit.
We can so easily fill in
The chalk outline of a body
With a narrative we have heard
So often on the evening news.

Even a clown with balloons

Parading with a large sign

Announcing no down payments

Until the first of the year

Only gets us to tap our brakes.

If you want more than a glance,

You need to do something exceptional,

Something extravagant.

Forget it, don't think

Of planting a tree for the victim—

It's too common nowadays.

Enough with the plastic flowers

And pinned photos—we already have

Too many faces on milk cartons.

Listen: spend some money.

Hire a belly dancer if you can,

Then get yourself a noisy band.

High school marching bands are the best.

Hire a group of men, not too young,

Neatly dressed in suits,

And instruct them to tie

A ribbon between two trees,

Then have them ceremoniously cut it.

Stand by a table with rows of cookies

And provide us with punch.

Then, when you sense we are ready,

In a weak but steady voice

Begin to tell us about him.

What was his name again?

And how old was he?

The Bougainvillea Asks

Again,
Why do you kiss your wife, turning to one side,
Curling up into a pile of leaves while she reads,
Adjusting her light on a book she can't put down?

The wind brings me the scent of wild sage.
I comb my hair with its scent. Join me tonight.
The wind tapping at your glass is me.
Listen:
My eyes flutter, all of them, clinging like you,
A stem away from whirling into a chaos.
O my dear, don't be afraid—
Think of the gaze flipping to the next page.

I have heard you murmur my name,
The music of my syllables.
What has to happen before you realize
What you must do?

Slant

The hissing of onion rings called him,
But he sat on the wet tiles instead.
The orders whirled on the stainless-steel wheel,
And a waitress from across the kitchen yelled:
"What's he doing on the floor like that?"

Across town a family of pickers also sat
While a school bus of field hands drove by.
They too were finished with crop picking.

When the factory workers elected to stop,
They didn't know what to do with their hands.
Some put them in their pockets, others propped
Their heads, a few stared at their palms,
Which made the foreman nervous, prompting him
To run into his office and hide behind a cabinet.

Something spread across the city like a prayer,
But the aisles in grocery stores were still full,
And the neighborhood lawns seemed well groomed,
Though weeds and crabgrass began to thrive.

Some people imagined more trash on the sidewalks.
Yet there was no earthquake or great fire of change.
Only the smallest tilting of the day could be sensed.

The price of fruit stayed the same for now.
The children of migrants stayed in their rooms.
The school nurse reported no nosebleeds.
Two bakeries didn't flip their signs to "Abierto."
The tortillas, pale and sweaty, were not delivered.
No one would be taking tickets at the theater.
The new off-ramp would stay closed a little longer.
On that first day nothing really big happened
That one could say was out of the ordinary.

La Gatita de Michoacán

We prefer
To use Ana Maria, though we must pick her up
And drive her home, her strong and slender wrists
Resting over her purse on the ride to our house.

We admit we would not be surprised to discover
A kid or two pulling at the skirt of our Ana Maria,
Yet we have never gone beyond her apartment door
Because she is quick to follow us back to our car.

The change she finds between the sofa's cushions
She stacks on the coffee table, and without being told
She pulls out our fridge and cleans our stained wall.
Imagine that!
Then at evening she stands ready to leave, neat,
Composed as if ready to start the day again,
Her strong and slender wrists resting over her purse.

The House in El Monte

He was not surprised the ivy grew
Where the chicken-wire fence once stood,
And a stump still marked the yard's end.
He stared at the rusty hinges of a screen door,
The screen grim as his aunt's death veil,
And recalled a room shrunk to a mattress
That pressed against a wall of stains.
His finger would follow a crack on the stucco,
Then another until he found a route out.
The stains on the ceiling grew into islands,
And the lumpy raft he shared with his sisters
Drifted while roaches squirmed around them.
He wormed between his sisters and slept.
The house was chicken-bone brittle
And had a creaking voice until dawn.

After his second knock a woman appeared,
Tilting her head to one side to see around him.
While he told her in his choppy Spanish
He had once lived in her house, she ordered

The two children hiding behind her legs

And peering at him to return to the kitchen.

When she turned her head to call her husband,

He said, "Mire, señora," pulling out a photo.

She reached for it, studying the family

Standing in front of her house, the same

Tilting TV antenna, the paint flaking off the door,

And at the bottom the dog's scratches.

She waited on her side of the threshold,

Scrutinizing a boy's face, then his,

Trying to match what in him had not changed,

But before he could see the bedroom wall

Where he had scratched with his fingernails,

She turned him away, closing the door,

Suspicious he was eyeing their belongings,

And locking the door latch as if to say,

"Déjenos en paz. No tenemos nada."

All That Passes for Him

The belly of a church is lit
With prayers, flickering eyes,
Then a cross stings like a whip.

Atcale

Taking the trade winds as its route,
A man-of-war headed to the New World,
And nights plagued the men, giving them
An endless sail to project their fears.
One morning a flock of seagulls circled,
And fish with wings darted out of the water,
              Skimming the surface.
The men cheered when they saw land.
They surrounded their camp with night fires,
Then a guard staring at the surf yelled: "Canoe!"
The soldiers rushed to the beach, spotting a figure.
              Some thought the savages were attacking,
But it was only an enormous turtle coming onto shore.
Some men shook their heads, walking back to their fires,
              But a few surrounded it,
Then one positioned his lance under its belly,
Rocking the turtle, and others joined in.
While the upside-down turtle wiggled its limbs,

One man said its oars were useless,
Unable to reach the water, so he drove
His sword down, severing its feet.
The turtle jerked its head in and out of its shell.
With its underside reflecting the moonlight,
A finger traced over its breastplate, the way
A captain charts his course with a compass:
In a distant country deeds were being drawn up,
Machetes were being forged, and the banks
Of rivers darkened in the ink of new maps.

Las Milpas de Anenecuilco

He heard dynamite, his boys had reached the plaza,
The pueblo was theirs, the garrison was next.
He rode, a rebel, a medium to voices, hearing
The common people who spotted him on a slope,
Riding through the villages in his state of Morelos,
Searching for a tin box that held his village's deeds,
The communal lands, signed by the viceroy of Spain.
He fought for the next harvest and that tin box,
Which held the planting seasons of his ancestors.

He recalled a curandera who saw his birthmark,
A handprint on his chest, and said he was cursed
Because it was the corn silk and Spain's branded seal
And would become a hand cutting free Zapatistas left
Dangling on a tree, the fruit of a splintered branch.

Birthday Party

In the morning he went to the market
And pointed at a papier-mâché donkey.
The woman behind the meat counter
Walked past the hooves of pigs,
Chopped bones with strips of flesh.
With a broom she poked the piñata off
A clothesline of dangling donkeys and goats.

The nylon rope burned his palm
As he jerked the piñata, strung up
And bouncing in the air. More children
Gathered while he stopped for the boy
Sent to fetch a bat from the garage.

In line, a girl of six stepped back,
Glancing down at her Sunday shoes,
Ignoring the hand pushing her on,
Stepping aside, watching the paper
Curls on the donkey's belly tremble.

★

"Take the bat, sweetheart. Take it.
The piñata is full of candy. Hit it."
Her father's voice was one of many,
A field of crows squawking at dusk,
Drawing others into a rising swirl.

The donkey jerked above the swinging bat,
Then a half-blindfolded boy jumped,
Landing a blow, knocking off a hoof,
A stream of candy, a rush of hands
Swooping up whatever glittered.

Perros y Muerte

Sunday: Father stuffed a bill in my pocket
And saw me out the door. I headed downtown,
Passing by the marked-down prices and displays,
And in Johnson's Hardware men stood by
The coffee machine brewing its next pot.
The butcher untied his apron. Lunchtime.
A dog slept by Art's Barbershop, which shared
A bathroom with the local bar, Los Ojos.
Art turned me to face the mirror and asked:
"How short does your old man want it?"
After trimming around my ear, he whispered:
"John Holmes," a porn star who made Art pinch
The inside of his thigh and brag: "See that?
It goes down to my knee." "Yeah, right!" I said.
While the dog sniffed at Art's glass door,
I heard footsteps coming from the bar.
A man staggered in, pressing his hand
Over a rib. His fingers were bloody.

He took an awkward step, then another, head-heavy,
Propped himself against the wall, then slid.
He sat, coughing between his choppy breaths.
Then, slapping the floor, he left
A handprint, red as the butcher's apron.
Art stood in a widening pool of blood
That gathered clumps of hair, gray stubs,
And mine, black curls, long as eyelashes.
When the sirens passed us, I ran out the door.
By then Art had turned the man on his back
And smoothed back a strand of hair touching his eye.
The whirling fan had caught the man's gaze,
And the dog scratching to get in held mine.

2.

I saw a dark bundle of blankets and yelled:

                    "Shit! My dog!"
I cut the engine of my motorcycle, thinking my dog
Had escaped from our backyard and run into the street.
A circle of neighbors had gathered in front of my house.
And one said: "It's dark, and look at him!
He's dressed in black. There's no moon, too."

Another shouted: "Some fuck hit Tony, and the fucker

Just kept going. Can you fuckin' believe that?"

I held his hand and asked if he could move his legs;

He wiggled his fingers, walking them down his side.

Keeping Tony warm with blankets was all we could do.

After they drove him away, I jumped on my bike.

I braked at each cross street, scanning driveways,

Studying cars driving too quickly, cars idling in lots,

And cars turning off their headlights when I passed.

All the neighborhood dogs barked as I raced by,

Hoping the car would circle back out of remorse.

My cracked tailpipe roared, "Where's that fucker?"

3.

After the bell set the house dogs in a dash, a whippet

Scraping its nails on the driveway got to me first.

As soon as the arm of the electric gate pulled back,

It jumped and nipped at my wrist, daring me to run.

With someone else's get-well card, I visited my friend,

Exceedingly sick, recently released from days of testing.

On his kitchen counter a banana softened, caved in,

A nightmare he had, a face wrapped with leaves spoke

Of a blacksmith, his father, whose iron glowed and hissed,

A rod steaming in a barrel and fixed in its form.

His dream clung like the ivy on his winter wall.

He sat on a plush carpet of shag, clapping for his dogs.

He reminded me how his prize whippet chased rabbits.

Once she got a scent, she dashed into the brush,

Reappearing with cuts on her face and shoulders,

Panting by his side, only to return to the chase,

Jumping to see over the brush, which was all around her.

As he spoke, his dogs, four in all, drew around him,

The gray whippet circling its spot and sighing before

Tucking itself by his side. My friend dozed off.

When I turned the doorknob, his dogs raised their heads,

Poised to dash out the door, vying to set the pace.

St. Francis

In a desert too hot and cold for most,
Where winds send trailer homes rolling
And drifting into sand dunes, you dug
And cemented a stand for your saint
Who protects all living creatures, even me
Who says deserts are only good for buzzards.

"Here the dust gathers everywhere,
And there is no avoiding it," you say
As you sweep your trailer's doorway clean,
Inviting me, your cousin, to stay for supper.

When I ask you why you put up your saint
And your house on its blocks here, you say:
"I step into this vista like a prayer.
I was just rehearsing before—I was like
A waiting suitor whose finger hovers
Over the doorbell, afraid to go on in."

Backyard

For Scott Francis

I

Her son watches from his window
The leaves of the walnut tree turn into bats,
Their eyes blind as the marbles under his bed.
When he turns toward his room, they appear again
On his wall, dark wings, outlined by the moon.
His finger traces where their faces would be
If they were not tucked under their wings.
Some tremble, opening their wings,
      A cry for flight.

II

Quietly, as she prayed at his funeral,
She pinches off the leaf of a geranium,
Holding it, a kerchief to grieve her son.
She walks through a garden of relatives,
Asking them to please stand and leave
Because she has to water the lawn.

III

The walnut tree's leaves were once a gift,

       Lavish, loosely worn,

        Now fallen.

    A crisp step,

A squirrel flips a leaf and finds

A walnut, then scurries into the shade.

The sky beyond the tree,

       A cage of branches,

Is hungry for the captive birds to fly.

IV

A breeze fills her curtains, the nets of night.

      She unbuttons her blouse

While the bougainvillea's eyes follow her

To the end of the stepping stones.

The leaf creeping, a tilting shadow points

      Her to a spider's arc.

The green that feeds on the underside of moist stones

      Thickens the air.

The First Day They Searched for a Mailbox

Reading "letter," thinking *carta,* she dropped hers
Into a trash bin labeled "litter," then a bee
Darted out of its swinging door. She double-checked,
Smelling a hamburger pattie. Her arm plunged in,
Then she helped her son squeeze half his torso
Into the green bin strapped to a lamp pole.
He dug deeper, spotting their stamp, a tiny flag.
She yanked him out by his belt when a car
Stopped to honk at them. She nudged him on
While ants zigzagged among the blades of grass
And drifted away from their scented trails.
He had vanished into the glare of a sidewalk,
Skipping and knowing that if he stepped on
A crack, he would break his mother's back.
At night the words of her letter reached her
Like the TV voices from the apartment next door
Until her letter hovered, a recited prayer,
The one she kneeled under before leaving León.

Santa Ana Winds

For Flavia

The wind that is
Famous for tossing eucalyptus trees
Scratched one of your window screens
With the bougainvillea's green thorns,
Then sneaked into your father's room,
Sly as fire,
Arousing the dust.

He clung to his bed sheets,
His mouth spent on cursing the wind,
The same one that showed up
At his funeral like an invited guest.
Jeff, who sells cars, shook
Your hand as if he had closed a deal.
The rest sat, hearing the wind shake
The funeral parlor's glass, insisting
It alone marked the seasons.

The night he died
A candy wrapper followed

The route grocery lists travel,

And the glue of his books yellowed,

Then cracked like a mind.

While you tried to close the window,

Feeling for it to give way,

You heard a howl for the not yet

Audible sirens you, too,

Would have to summon.

Panorama Fire, 1980

Yesterday, the fire raised its voice,

A crackling and hissing that fed on the land.

Like a boy in full stride, panting, it ran through

               A block of homes.

Firemen on their walkie-talkies called for hoses

While neighbors pointed to a line of flames that rolled

With the hillside and swallowed the tall grass with ease,

Spitting out clouds shifting in the wind.

    It leveled the block to smoking pipes.

    They have let residents return,

And driveways divide ash mounds.

               One woman walks,

Hand over mouth, wondering what is left to salvage.

A man who has spent the morning poking through the ash

Cleans his sunglasses, and another steps into his garage

And turns, imagining the walls around him,

Spotting a sledgehammer's head, recalling his tool rack.

A doorknob points the way to the kitchen;

He walks past the washing machine and dryer,

Heaps of melted steel and plastic,

Pausing by a sink held up by its drainpipe.

His wife is done with the digging,

An exercise in looking for what is not there,

And leans on the chimney's shoulder.

The fire's teeth combed through the grassy hills

And left them black as a stink bug.

The scorched statue of a squirrel is hollow,

                Still in stride.

A tree's ends are pokers, ashy white.

              Mats of grass puff;

The stalks of yucca plants

And cacti are scattered on the ground,

But the odor of wild sage lingers

While under the bellies of stones, insects hide,

           Droning like power lines,

Electricity rising out of the ground.

On a hill barren as a reef, black ants set out

For their trails, their bodies an armor against the sun.

A red-tailed hawk circles,

           Casting his shadow in a valley

Where bees teem around their beehives, man-made,

Once white boxes, set in rows.

One is still smoking;

Its bees hover, lost like strangers in a train station,

But others dart to a familiar entrance,

Approach out of habit,

And search, suspended at an opening, a panorama.

Her Household

1.

Switching on the light in the garage,
She heard a rat run from beam to beam,
But she only saw its tail disappear.
She stood holding a basket of dirty clothes.
If she got a broom, she could not face it,
If she got poison, she would worry about her kids,
If she set a few traps and caught it,
She would be the one to find it,
Gutted, blood-dried, eyes dark as tacks.
Quickly throwing the clothes in the washer,
She ran with the basket over her head,
Seeing her breath race in front of her.
She wondered if winter would make it discreet.
She wondered if spring would bring it birth.

2.

She wipes the kitchen counter off,

Trying not to look at the floor,

Trying not to worry that someone

Might come and notice the Cheerios

And the tomato spots on the floor.

On her knees she cleaned that floor yesterday,

But it's dirty again, mocking her,

So she moves from the cupboard to the table,

    Ready to snap at the kids.

All the work she put into dinner matters,

    She says, dishing out a plate:

"Just eat without making a fuss for once."

At night her blanket swells,

    A wave ending at her chin,

A receding dream pulls at her

While her recipes float around her.

3.

The night curtains hold her curves

Until the glare of morning wakes her.

The hands in her mirror slide on a dress,

Its pattern of lilies

    Smelling of daily chores.

    Her glass flashes a grin:

    "See you in the kitchen."

    Yet, she does not see her twin

    In the bottom of a pan this day.

4.

So, her sofa needs new cushions

And her living room needs a makeover.

The welcome mat has a bad attitude,

Rolling up one of its four tongues,

And the clock has lost its second hand.

So what, her coffee table has a drinking problem

And has the water stains to show for it.

She walks through her crayon house,

Laughing at herself, a pinned-up drawing,

Slipping from its magnet's hold.

Kiss

As you spoke, a cricket sang
In my tumbleweed heart,
And wild sage surrounded us.

When your lips touched me,
A bird felt a fountain
With its fluttering wings.

Two-Timer

True, Debby was pure as Weber bread,
And he couldn't take homegirls anymore,
In particular La Cherry who almost sucked
His Adam's apple straight out of his neck
With one of those vacuum-loving kisses.
If La Cherry found out about his marshmallow
Of love, she'd blow, a Cherry bomb.
She'd cut and watch him drip like Heinz.

Still, he was sick of that white makeup,
Jet lipstick, you know, the vampira look.
Yet, La Cherry in moonlight would do
The nasty, holding tight all the way.
He would stride through the school quad
With those dark hickeys, rich as chocolate.

Undetectable

On Saturdays I found myself at Fairmont,
The city's hidden park, shaded by oleanders
That kept the freeway drivers from peering,
Then swerving in their lanes.
I wiggled my fingers over a bench's edge.
"You're still there, though no one can see you."
How I lost my thumb was not important,
Only that my right hand groped for doorknobs,
Fumbled for phones, and settled for clumsy handshakes.
Walking home I pinched off a few rosebuds
And snapped a dangling branch from a sycamore.
Later, I balanced a book with my right hand.
While I faced the pages, an odd idea struck me.
The next day I walked to the public library,
Entered, and lost myself in the rows of books.
When no one was looking, I pulled one out,
Flipped through it, trying to find a page,
The right page to cut and crumple in my pocket.
I glanced down the shelf, checking over my back,
Feeling for my pocketknife, deciding I should make

A clean, undetectable cut.

I couldn't take just any page.

I needed the essential page.

"That's what I'll do," I said,

Proceeding to check out several books.

Poetry was too easy,

And long novels could lose dozens of pages.

Then I found a book of translated stories

By a poet from Buenos Aires.

I was happy for a short time.

Each story had an irreplaceable page.

I kept those pages, stapling one after another,

But after rereading my homemade handout,

I had the uneasy feeling they were forming a story,

Independent of their original ones.

The pages were conspiring against me,

Linking inscrutable patterns.

Yet I kept checking out books from the library,

But not as many because I had begun to lose interest

In finding the page that would irrevocably change

The story once my blade had sliced down its heart.

Nido

With someone on either side of him holding his hands,
The boy runs, faster than he can go by himself,
His feet skipping above the ground,
And over him flies a window that frames
    His grandpa's face.

    Now that the boy's father is dead,
His grandpa shows up more often, mentioning how much
He had to pay so his son could have a decent burial.
Outside the boy counts the stepping-stones
Taking him to his father's grave marker.

    The grandpa throws off his cap;
He's hungry and sits himself down.
The boy spots on the screen door a beetle
Showing off its hairy legs, its yellow-spotted belly.

His shadow spreads across the lawn to the boy.
    He forgot to rake the leaves.
With the quickness of a grasshopper's leap,
The grandpa strikes the boy.

★

　　His face stings as he walks
To a porch that is leaf cluttered, reeling.
The window fades when the kitchen light goes off,
And the lawn widens until there is no hiding place.

Grocery Stores

I

He hid in the public library, reading
Of a princess who played a harp for a giant
Who lived in a castle above the clouds
And had caged her for his pleasure.
The princess sang from behind her bars
Until the giant, dressed in green,
Slept, unaware of a boy's footsteps,
A boy who had found a way into his castle.
He so wanted to be that boy and rescue her.

II

He sat in front of a TV screen
With a sweetness on his tongue,
The glue of S & H Green Stamps.
The cashiers would hand them sheets
Of stamps that he licked onto pages,
The books they collected like notes,

Then spent at the redemption center
Where the strips on the air vents waved,
And the waxed floor spread its luster.

III

At Lucky's, a nearby grocery store,
A manager reached for his mother's elbow,
And asked her to empty her purse.
Her purse jerked open when she pulled away.
He ran and peered from behind parked cars.
One day he would rescue her, a woman
Dependent on the State for welfare,
The coupons, the food packed in boxes
Labeled with a government's blue shield
She had him rip before each trash day.

IV

The wheels of their stolen cart whined
Because they had to walk the following weeks
To Staters, a grocery store two miles away,
But that also ended when he discovered
The Polaroids someone had spread across

The white loaves of Wonder Bread,

The glossy snapshots of a naked body.

A woman stretched out on a green sofa,

Her privates, brush-thick and leaf shaped.

Under the fluorescent lights she gleamed

Like the sleek side of a cardboard display.

A lady wearing her Sunday hat caught his ear

And said: "Come with me, you dirty boy."

V

Who would drive them to Ralph's,

Whose tomatoes were being sprayed

Until tears ran down their sides,

And items glided to a smiling boxboy?

His mother never had to check

Her coin purse twice in his TV ads

And look around like the day a lady

Behind them handed the cashier a dollar

And fifty cents they didn't have.

The lady smiled while they walked out,

And the speakers raved about markdowns.

An empty plastic bag tumbled,

Hitting a car's grill as the driver

Circled, finding a space by the doors,

And seeing its blinker click yellow,

A yellow pumping like a chest,

He knew he had to climb the beanstalk

That would sprout from under his bed

And rescue the princess from her prison,

An enormous birdcage made of gold.

As a reward he would receive a golden egg

And make his way down the beanstalk,

Feeling it slip when the clouds gave way

To patches of farmland, not so much

The pages of a fairy tale as of a quilt

His mother made from hand-me-downs.

A Charged-Up Apricot Tree

The overripe fruit taps the ground,
                    Taut as a drum.
The neighbor's cat sits on the wall,
Crouching among the drooping branches,
The baited traps for winged mice.

The spoiling scent of the fruit mocks
A family of pickers on their circuit.
For whom else does He play and scatter
A decaying sheet of music on the ground?

Ofelia

For OCD

I. WORK CAMP

She sits
In a chicken coop
Turned camp
And nurses her twins,
Blossom hungry and plump.
She walks between the rows
Of chicken coops,
And the camp eyes part their curtains,
Sheets strung up with clothespins.
Her can opener ran out of food,
So lock your door, Anna,
And play deaf, Ampara and Martha.
She picks a few oranges
Among the frost-bitten trees,
Their leaves tucked in,
Dark branches.

2. HITCHHIKING

She travels the routes of gas pumps
And 7-11 diaper runs,
Leaving the lemons under the wet sun,
The ditches, and the splinters
Of ladders.
Her eyes are in his rearview mirror
When the yellow line veers
And sheds its skin;
Patting the seat, he asks her to sit
Up front with him, and her girls
Are drowned out by the tires' drone.
At the next stop
They will vanish behind a wall
Of eucalyptus, Santa Ana windbreaks,
Or stay in a gas station's restroom.
She will hold her girls until curses turn
To squealing tires.

3. THEIR GARDEN

Her girls' eyes are with the bees
Hovering among the blossoms.

They lie on a blanket
Made from old flour sacks.
One has learned to roll onto her stomach.
Ofelia walks between the rows,
Brushes against a web heavy with dew,
And glitters.
She checks if they are alone,
Singing so they can hear her voice.
Her song is a nursery, a grove
Of oranges not yet oranges,
Sweetening.

Gatekeepers

1.

A crow gliding over a ravine was
The sign his eyes were waiting for.
They thought they were ready to cross.

The tumbleweed listening to a cricket
And seeing a line of ants snaking in
Was the figure of his younger sister,
Huddled by him, asking for a campfire.

They made it as far as a roadside store
And held their hands over the electric coils.
When asked if they were going to buy anything,
Their tongues broke off into halves
And fell to the floor like Popsicles.

2.

My father says I was born to translate
What he could only nod to for years.
He also says that God made a mistake

By blurring out his eyes first because
He can hear her asking for a blanket.

She saw a church adorned with hipbones,
Sun-bleached, and beautiful as curved jewelry.
She dreamt of its wide doors, and after dipping
Her finger in His palm, she felt His warmth.

My father says that cactus needles fly
And burn like the memory of lost ones,
Then he tells me I was born to study
The sand trails and notice when footsteps
Drag and turn to knee and handprints.
Those are ones I need to follow, he says.

Diapers

INS officers raided a building, taking twelve illegal aliens into custody. The owner was cited for employing workers without proper identification.

1. RAID

Ernesto's boot heels are wild hooves

Being roped in, left bound in the air.

Carmen, slow-footed, nauseous with child,

Fights them off by swinging her purse.

"Pinche cabrones saben hablar español

Cuando nos van a arrestar," she says

As her voice is drowned out by a row

Of washing machines on their rinse cycle.

Like a cat spooked out of a trash bin,

Sal runs into the street.

Chorus: ¡Chingado!

2. A GIRL AND HER FATHER

We were driving through town, Mama,

Right by where people pick up the bus

When this man jumps right in front of us.

Dad hit the brakes. His eyes got this big, Mama.

He was running from the law, that's for sure.

Just be glad no one got hurt, mija.

Try not to think about it anymore, mija.

We won't go that way again, that's for sure.

3. THE FACTORY

Two of the old-timers talked about unions:

"A trabajar, porque hablar de las uniones

Sólo trae la migra de nuevo."

4. A YOUNG MOTHER

Can you imagine how many diapers

We went through with the twins?

The disposable ones were way too expensive,

So we switched to cloth. They were great. No,

We didn't wash them. Thank God, we had a service.

We just put the dirty ones in plastic bags,

And they picked them up and dropped off clean ones

Right on our porch every two weeks.

It made things so much easier. And you know,

We didn't have to worry about those summer rashes

Because their little bottoms could breathe better.

If you can afford the service, just do it.

Or at least do it for the first six months.

It's even good for the environment.

5. JEFE

No son gallinas

Esperando un huevo.

¡A trabajar!

Chorus: ¡Chingado!

I Have Two Sisters

When Flavia goes on a date, I have to
Accompany her, though I am younger.
Once I caught her praying to a saint
And tying a ribbon on his rope belt.
She will untie the ribbon after marriage.

When holding up nylon stockings,
She exclaims only whores wear them.
She often complains I walk too fast
And asks: "¿Adónde vas tan rápido?"

My other sister, Gloria, complains
I spend too much time looking back.
"Shit, did you drop something, or what?"
She is a curtain being drawn out
By a breeze from our house and ways.

She is not afraid of breaking rules.
She presses against her boyfriend's body.
The garden's dampness creeps up their legs,
Turning them into tilting shadows.

★

I, like any middle child, have to remind
The one too close to the old ways
And the one caught up with her youth
To act like sisters at least for my sake.

Mojados

There he goes again, standing on the corner,
Wrapping his cheap carnations in cellophane.
He waves them like it was pinche Día de las Madres.
Was that him the other day leaving flyers
Advertising a lawn service on our porches?
Is he the guy that neighbors say can mow
A block of lawns on a Saturday afternoon?

The sister he crossed with now pushes a cart
Of paletas made out of mango, coconut, y limón.
She rings her bell up and down our barrio,
Making the kids tug at their abuelitas' purses
And dogs charge their chain-link fences.

                              I bet
La Virgen y todos los santos are watching over them
So that her ice doesn't melt and his flowers
Don't dry up and fall to the ground like the petals
By those homemade crosses that litter our roads.

My Backyard Neighbor

Gloria watched the cars cruise past a motel with a neon sign
Flickering, "Electric Heat." The cars lowered their windows
Until a pair of eyes surfaced. The local mariachi band,
Made up of drunks, toured the restaurants and bugged the young couples
Who sat kissing on the park benches. Once, on her way home, Gloria
Found a vendor roasting corn and warmed her hands over the coals.
She smelled like a pile of burnt husks, making me hungry.

                                                      At Gloria's,
A converted garage behind us, I found empty cans of condensed
Milk on the floor. She asked for an extra cup of rice or a slice
Of government-issued cheese, so yellow we joked the police
Used it yesterday to fence off a crime scene. Later that day
My mother had me sit while she slammed cupboards, checking to see
What I had stolen for Gloria, asking: "Does she have viejos
Over there?" Weeks later headlights roamed our streets, and a roach
Wiggling its antennas at me wondered: "La migra? Is la migra
Deporting Gloria? Who turned her in?" My mother stood over me,
Saying: "That woman had you stealing. It was a matter of time
Before she had viejos, dirty viejos looking into our windows."

I thought of the men who stood outside motel doors, combed their hair

In the windows, and then lit up. I ran out. Her house was empty.

I ran toward the park, toward the odor of roasted corn.

If Gloria was not at her corner, I was sure she would return.

I was sure her john would bring her across the border again.

Tío

Cuerpos que se abren paso entre otros cuerpos.
  —Octavio Paz

As a boy
You wanted to wear a dandelion
And let your friends' eyes drift
And fix on your mother's flower.
When they asked you to play soccer,
You would not, not that day.
You were a son without a mother then,
Showing the imprint of her beauty.

Recently a doctor asked you:
"Take it off. Remember, you're a diabetic."
When the doctor rolled down your sock,
Your stubbornness turned green,
A cut, unattended, blackening.

You tell me you are
A rocking horse without a floor,
Dangling from a wire branch
Like a Christmas ornament.

Tío, a corner of this poem
Was amputated as you reminded me

Of my father, lying on his bed, pointing

To his plastic vials, colorful pills

That mixed on his palette until only

One color remained, drying up.

    You too live on your bed now,

Fixed as an envelope's stamp.

The ripped triangle of paper

Buried in my pocket grew like lint

Until I put it in a photo box.

In my youth you waxed a Thunderbird

And flashed by with your dragonfly eyes.

You were my father's right shadow.

When they changed your sheets,

I saw your imprint or was that

    My father's as well?

Your mattress sagged in the middle,

Holding your outline, an orbit

Surrounding the force of another body.

    Tío, if only your mattress

Could be a chest and inhale,

Losing its imprinted figures.

Hiding under a Bus

His coyote led him through a corridor,
Opening to a desert, and when the flowers
Of the saguaros opened at dusk, he saw
A woman giving birth on the sand.
At dawn the agents circled in their plane,
Loud as flies, hovering over the border,
"Mercy flights" the locals called them.

After checking a clipboard, a guard
Had him wait alongside an idling bus.
The voices of inmates filtered through
The bus's undercarriage where he had hid
When the guards were distracted. "¡Qué milagro!"
Once far away from the detention center,
He would let go at a stop and roll away.
                              "Ay, qué sencillo."

He had wedged his feet and hooked his arms,
But once the bus headed to the gate,
The road's mouth drew him in, swallowed,

Its receding tongue licking his eyelids.
He woke to the swaying of a lightbulb,
The odor of embroidered pillows, carpets,
And old curtains, then a sweet stench,
A bowl of guayabas left in a corner.

He was in his aunt's house again,
And no one was surprised to see him,
No one minded that lingering odor.
The white doilies lay on the sofa's arms
Like waxy flowers under the moonlight.
His Aunt Chela joined him on the sofa,
Showing him the pages of an album,
Its plastic sheets reflecting the light.
Cousins he had not seen since childhood
Greeted him with gifts, a spun top,
A leopard's mask. "¡Qué extraño!"
His relatives talked around him, referring
To stories they were fond of retelling:
"Sí, me recuerdo. Sí, me recuerdo."
One relative stared into her cup,
Nodding at the dark rings under her eyes.
He got up to press his palm against

A window, trying to feel the day's heat,
Realizing he had to leave again.
He knew how far night would take him
And left, relying on his memory of routes
Not heavily traveled in the summer months.
After roaming their streets and alleys,
A pack of dogs saw him to the outskirts,
Then barked at the gravel under his feet,
A sound weaving through the desert brush.
"Allá está la frontera, allá está."

GLOSSARY

abierto.   Open.
abuelitas.   Grandmothers.
atcale.   Canoe.
calavera.   Skull.
carta.   Letter.
chicas.   Girls.
chingado.   Screwed, fucked.
curandera.   Medicine woman.
gatita.   Kitten.
golpe.   Punch or blow.
jefe.   Boss.
limón.   Lemon.
mamasita.   Little mama.
masa.   Dough.
La Migra (inmigracíon).   Immigration officers or service.
mija.   Daughter.
milpas.   Cornfields.
mojados.   Wetbacks.
nido.   Nest.
paletas.   Popsicles.
señorita.   Young lady.
tío.   Uncle.
vampira.   Vampire.
viejos.   Old men.
Zapatistas.   The followers of Emiliano Zapata, a revolutionary leader.

A trabajar, porque hablar de las uniones sólo trae la migra de nuevo.
   (Back to work because talk of the unions only brings immigration officers back.)

¿Adónde vas tan rápido?   (Where are you going so fast?)

Allá está la frontera, allá está.   (Over there is the border, over there.)

Ay, qué sencillo.   (How simple.)

Cuerpos que se abren paso entre otros cuerpos.   (Bodies who open a way into others.) This line is taken from "Más Allá del Amor," a poem from *Girasol,* by Octavio Paz.

Déjenos en paz. No tenemos nada.   (Leave us in peace. We have nothing.)

El Caballo de Cortés.   (The Horse of Cortés.)

La Virgen y todos los santos.   (The Virgin and all the saints.)

Mire, señora.   (Look, lady.)

No son gallinas esperando un huevo. ¡A trabajar!   (You are not hens waiting for an egg. Get to work!)

Perros y Muerte.   (Dogs and Death.)

Pinche cabrones saben hablar español cuando nos van a arrestar.   (You motherfuckers know Spanish when you are going to arrest us.)

Pinche Día de las Madres.   (Fucking Mother's Day.)

¡Qué extraño!   (How strange!)

¡Qué milagro!   (What a miracle!)

Sí, me recuerdo.   (Yes, I remember.)

ACKNOWLEDGMENTS

I would like to thank the editors of the following periodicals and books for accepting and publishing my poetry: "Backyard," *South Dakota Review* 34, no. 4 (1996): 30–31; "Birthday Party" (as "Backyard Party"), *Luna* 1, no. 2 (1999): 211–12; "The First Day They Searched for a Mailbox" and "The House in El Monte," *The Bayou Review* (fall 2000): 26, 38; "La Gatita de Michoacán," *Kestrel* 16 (fall 2000–spring 2001): 140; "The Ghost of Sal" and "Panorama Fire, 1980" (as "August"), *El Andar* (winter 1998): 8, 35; "Grandma Taught Me to Respect You," *Bloomsbury Review* 15, no. 4 (1995): 9; "Shrine," "Diapers," and "Hiding under a Bus," *Voices of Latino Culture: Readings from Spain, Latin America, and the United States,* 2d edition, ed. Daniel S. Whitaker (Dubuque, Ia.: Kendall/Hunt, 1996, 2002): 201–6; "Mojados" and "My Backyard Neighbor" (as "Back Street Neighbor"), *Free Lunch* no. 25 (2000): 10–11; "Slant" and "Nido," *Colorado Review* 27, no. 2 (2000): 25–27; "Two-Timer," *Touching the Fire: Fifteen Poets of Today's Latino Renaissance,* ed. Ray Gonzalez (New York: Anchor/Doubleday, 1998): 114.

ABOUT THE AUTHOR

Juan Delgado lives in San Bernardino with his wife, Jean, and their three children, Anna, Marco, and Clara. He is a professor of English and assistant to the provost at California State University, San Bernardino. He was born in Guadalajara, Mexico, but he has lived most of his life in California. He received his M.F.A. from the University of California, Irvine, where he was a Regents Fellow. In 1990 his book *A Change of Worlds* was awarded first place in a chapbook contest sponsored by Embers Press. Four years later, *Green Web* was the winning manuscript for the Contemporary Poetry Series and was published by the University of Georgia Press. His second chapbook, *Working on It,* is a series of sonnets about vatos (homeboys). The collection is part of the Chicano Chapbook Series, which is edited by Gary Soto. In his next book, *El Campo,* he collaborated with the painter Simon Silva to create a series of paintings and poems that dramatizes the hardships of farmworkers and immigrants working in the United States.